Great Inventions
of the 20th Century

Great Inventions
of the 20th Century

By Peter Jedicke

CHELSEA HOUSE
PUBLISHERS
An imprint of Infobase Publishing

Scientific American: Great Inventions of the 20th Century

Chelsea House
An imprint of Infobase Publishing
132 West 31st Street
New York NY 10001

ISBN-10: 0-7910-9048-5

ISBN-13: 978-0-7910-9048-0

Library of Congress Cataloging-in-Publication Data
Jedicke, Peter.
  Scientific American. Great inventions of the 20th century / Peter Jedicke.
    p. cm.
  Includes bibliographical references and index.
  ISBN 0-7910-9048-5 (hc)
  1. Inventions—Juvenile literature. 2. Technology—History—20th century—
Juvenile literature. I. Title. II. Title: Great inventions of the 20th century.
  T48.J44 2006
  609'.04—dc22   2006014773

Chelsea House books are available at special discounts when purchased
in bulk quantities for businesses, associations, institutions, or sales
promotions. Please call our Special Sales Department in New York at
(212) 967-8800 or (800) 322-8755.

You can find Chelsea House books on the World Wide Web at
http://www.chelseahouse.com

Series designed by Gilda Hannah
Cover designed by Takeshi Takahashi

Printed in the United States of America

Bang GH 10 9 8 7 6 5 4 3 2 1

This book is printed on acid-free paper.

All links and Web addresses were checked and verified to be correct at
the time of publication. Because of the dynamic nature of the Web, some
addresses and links may have changed since publication and may no
longer be valid.

Contents

CHAPTER ONE

On the Road

Believe it or not, the giant crawler at Cape Canaveral that carries the space shuttle to the launch pad rides on a gravel road. Well-built roads made of dirt and gravel have supported horses and heavy loads for thousands of years. At the beginning of the twentieth century, almost all the roads in the United States were dirt or gravel. However, such roads are too dusty when the weather is dry and too muddy when it's wet. Also, they don't hold up well to fast-moving traffic. That's not a problem for the Cape Canaveral crawler, because it takes about 3 hours to cover the 3 miles (5 kilometers) to the launch pad.

It's not easy to give a road a proper hard surface. The surface needs to be strong and smooth but not slippery, even in the rain. One day in 1901, a businessman in Great Britain named E. P. Hooley noticed a spot on a road where someone had accidentally spilled **tar** on the gravel surface. Tar is a thick, gooey liquid often used to seal roofs or the wooden hulls of boats. Hooley noticed that to make the spill less sticky, small pebbles had been sprinkled over it. Hooley saw that the road was not dusty at all, and it occurred to him that this would be a good idea for building better roads. Hooley's company started producing a mix of tar and crushed slag from metal furnaces to spread

This section of road was improved by building a tarmac surface early in the twentieth century.

on top of gravel roads. He called this invention "tar macadam," or "**tarmac**" for short. Throughout the twentieth century, tarmac was used to build roads all over North America and all around the world.

Safety First

Just as important as the surface of roads are the safety features. The most famous safety feature is the cat's-eye. Percy Shaw worked as a road builder in England in the 1930s. One foggy night, as he was driving along, there was a dangerous curve in the road ahead. A cat sitting on the fence at the side of the road turned to look at his car, and the headlights were reflected in the cat's eyes. As he rounded the curve, Shaw had the idea to manufacture small glass reflectors and set them into the road. He decided to call these human-made reflectors cat's eyes. The reflectors even clean themselves because Shaw built them in a very shallow depression in the road so that car tires would splash water on them when it rained. There are now millions of them on roads all over the world.

Safety features are also built into cars themselves, although manufacturers usually resist including expensive features in their car designs. Safety glass is a good example. The windshields on early cars often shattered in minor accidents and caused terrible injuries. Then, in 1903, a French chemist named Edouard Benedictus reached for a glass flask on a shelf and knocked it over by mistake. It fell and broke, but he noticed that the pieces remained stuck together. Looking at the flask closely, he realized that a sticky chemical had dried on the inside of the glass. Benedictus went to work immediately in his laboratory and came up with a way to coat the glass with a thin layer of plastic

Cat's-eyes and reflective paint strips brilliantly mark this highway curve.

so that it wouldn't break into shards. Although his invention was used in goggles during World War I, it wasn't until 1927 that car manufacturers started to use safety glass in automobiles. Eventually, the U.S. government insisted that at least the front windshield of every car be made of layered safety glass.

Car Parts

The first automobiles in the late nineteenth century were hand-made. This is how wagons and carriages had always been built, but spare parts for automobiles were more complex than for wagons and carriages. Spare parts that had to be made one at a time to fit each car were very inconvenient. Cadillac of Detroit was the first manufacturer to make cars using identical parts. There was a dramatic demonstration of this advantage in England in 1908, when a car dealer named Frederick Bennet entered three Cadillacs in a race. Bennet had the cars completely taken apart in front of the audience. The hundreds of parts were then mixed up, and the three cars were rebuilt out of each other's parts. The cars ran perfectly, right off the starting line and into history.

Of all the inventions that went into automobiles in the twentieth century, perhaps the most famous is the V-8 engine. The

BUTTON COPY

Soon after cat's-eyes were invented, the U.S. government added the idea of reflective signs to the official rules for highway safety. For many years, the letters on highway signs had dozens of little reflective dots attached to them. This was called button copy. The buttons worked the same way cat's-eyes did. Button copy gave highway signs a unique look. By the 1980s, however, manufacturers figured out how to make reflective beads so tiny that they could be spread across a sheet like paint. Signs made from reflective sheets are much less expensive than button copy. So by the end of the twentieth century, no new button copy signs were being installed.

The first generation of traffic lights had only two lamps, unlike the three lamps in modern lights.

whole idea behind an internal-combustion engine is that a piston gets pushed by hot gases expanding rapidly inside a cylinder. For more power, it was necessary to either design larger cylinders or have more of them in the same engine. Putting many cylinders in a row was a pretty obvious solution, but it made for a long, narrow engine. The V-8 has two rows of four cylinders each, arranged at an angle to make the engine fit neatly under the hood of a car. Big V-8 engines were powerful and popular, especially in the United States.

Dealing with Congestion

As more and more people drove cars, the roads began to fill up, and traffic became a monstrous problem. Wider roads helped carry more cars, but that just made the traffic problem worse at intersections. The original solution was to have a policeman directing traffic, but that was dangerous and very hard work for the police. The modern traffic light, which most of us take for granted today, was actually invented in several steps. First, in Salt Lake City in 1912, there was a traffic light with just red and green lamps, controlled by a police officer at the side of the intersection. A bell would ring as a warning that the light was about to change! The yellow lamp was added in 1920 by William Potts, an inventive policeman in Detroit.

Another way to prevent collisions at road crossings is to build bridges to carry roads over each other. Arthur Hale, an engineer, drew the first modern cloverleaf junction in 1915 and received a patent for his invention. With the construction of just a single bridge, traffic in a cloverleaf can go in any direction without crossing other traffic. Still, the first cloverleaf was not built until 1928 in Woodbridge, New Jersey. Many variations of the classic cloverleaf have been tried since then. Imagine traveling on an interstate highway with traffic lights instead of junctions!

Streamlined Bridges

Roads would be used very little if they ended at every river or lake. To enable travelers to cross over, engineers have been building bridges for thousands of years. New materials and techniques in the twentieth century meant that bridges were taller, longer, and safer—usually. In 1940, a suspension bridge similar

U.S. HIGHWAYS

There's a saying from ancient times that "all roads lead to Rome." But in the modern world, a network of highways that goes in all directions is a better idea. In 1925, the U.S. government decided to create a network of highway numbers that carried on across state lines and, in some cases, right across the continent. U.S. 1, for instance, went from the Canadian border in Maine all the way to the southern tip of Florida. Another famous highway was Route 66 from Chicago to Los Angeles. A new network of freeways, called the Interstate Highway System, eventually replaced the U.S. route numbers as the nation's most important road system.

A freeway cloverleaf allows traffic to flow in any direction without stopping, but the design requires a large expanse of land.

to the famous Golden Gate Bridge was built at Tacoma Narrows, Washington. However, under the gentle arch of the suspension cables, the beautiful center span of the bridge collapsed on

These modern bridges in Hong Kong have been designed to withstand both the steady forces of wind and occasional storms.

November 7, 1940, just a few months after construction was complete. It was not the weight of the traffic or some tragic mistake in construction, but simply the wind that twisted the roadway of the bridge and brought it down. Although the wind was not as powerful as a tornado or hurricane, it made the roadway flutter and eventually tore it apart.

Some engineers responded to this challenge by building bridges with even more steel to make them strong enough not to twist when the wind pushes. Yet a more elegant approach was to design the bridge so that moving air could flow smoothly over and under without making the roadway flutter at all. This meant the surface could be much thinner and actually have more in common with an airplane wing than with a traditional bridge. European engineers have favored this type of design since the 1960s. The Humber Bridge in England has a roadway like this and was the longest suspension bridge in the world from 1981 until 1998.

CHAPTER TWO

At Home

Roads end in driveways, and driveways lead home. That's where inventions make the most difference—right where you live. Instead of shipping and storing ice to cool a room, for instance, air-conditioning made it possible to have just the right amount of cool air when it was needed. Mechanical equipment that uses a machine to suck heat out of air was invented in stages, like so many other things. Credit for the biggest steps goes to an engineer named Willis H. Carrier. Carrier had been quiet and shy as a boy. His mother helped him learn about fractions by cutting apples into equal pieces. He worked very hard so that he could study engineering, but throughout his life, he always focused on finding useful applications for his ideas.

Just after graduating from Cornell University, Carrier was thinking about how to make cool air while waiting at a train station in the fog. At that time, the best way to make cool air was to aim a fan over a block of ice. Carrier realized that the secret to better air cooling was to let droplets of water condense from the air like fog. In Carrier's invention, the air is blown over cold refrigerator coils. There is a gas sealed inside the coils, which is pumped out of the air conditioner and then forced to change to a liquid by the same pump. So, the gas absorbs heat from inside

This demonstration of an air conditioner shows a spray of cold mist and ice on the coils that carry the heat-absorbing gas.

the air conditioner and gives that heat back when it is outside. Meanwhile, the water droplets have condensed out of the air and are drained away. The dry, cool air is blown out of the air conditioner, which lowers the temperature in the room. Heat is energy, which cannot be created or destroyed, but the overall effect of the air conditioner is to transfer heat energy from inside the room outdoors.

In early designs, the chemical inside the sealed coils was **ammonia**, which is a hazardous substance. In 1928, another Cornell University engineering graduate named Thomas Midgley developed a whole family of new chemicals based on chlorine, fluorine, and carbon. Called **CFCs**, these chemicals don't harm people, despite being made of dangerous gases. (This is like the case of ordinary table salt, which is composed of sodium and chlorine, two very hazardous materials.) CFCs were soon used in air conditioners around the world, but in the 1970s, it was discovered that CFCs linger when they escape to the air. This is a serious problem because the CFCs destroy **ozone**, a chemical high in Earth's atmosphere. People need ozone as a shield from harmful ultraviolet light coming from the sun. In the twenty-first century, other chemicals are used in air conditioners instead of CFCs.

At first, air-conditioning was only used in factories where heat and humidity were a problem. Then, large systems were added to department stores and theaters to attract customers on hot summer days. It wasn't until 1928 that Carrier's company offered a small air-conditioning unit for homes called the "Weathermaker." Sales increased dramatically after World War II, and today, three out of four homes in the United States have air-conditioning.

Sanitation

Cool air was a wonderful convenience, but clean water was a necessity. Sanitation was the main reason why deadly diseases such as dysentery, cholera, and typhoid were stopped dead in

FAMILY BUSINESS

Many famous household names began with an inventor in the family. For instance, the vacuum cleaner was invented by James Murray Spangler in 1906, but it was his cousin and partner, William Hoover, whose name was on the best-known home cleaning invention of the century. In 1949, Frank Zamboni invented the rolling ice shaver that he and his brothers sold to ice rinks everywhere. Look for the Zamboni machine next time you go to a hockey game. Another example is Candido Jacuzzi, who developed a bathtub with water jets built right into it in 1968. Candido's sons ran their family business until 1979, and the name is still used even though the family no longer owns the company.

At a water-treatment plant, two sanitation technicians take a sample of the water so it can be tested.

their tracks. Credit for achieving this in 1919 goes to Abel Wolman and Linn Enslow, chemical engineers in Maryland. They knew that since 1908, chlorine had been added to the water-supply system of a city in New Jersey. Chlorine was a well-known poison. It was also the chemical used in gas attacks during World War I. Scientists were sure it would kill the **bacteria** that caused those fearful diseases, too. A tiny amount of chlorine mixed into the water was enough, but no one was sure exactly how much was best. Even a little bit too much chlorine makes water smell very unpleasant. Wolman and Enslow came up with the correct formula, so every time you take a drink of water, you prove that they were right. Millions of lives around the world have been saved since.

After a disease outbreak in 1992 in India, Ashok Gadgil took another step in making water cleaner. Ashok Gadgil knew that ultraviolet light, which packs more energy than the colors of light that you can see, would also kill bacteria. With so many people in the world living in areas where there were no large antipollution plants to chlorinate the water, Gadgil thought something more portable would be useful. His invention is called "UV Waterworks." By shining powerful ultraviolet light on a tray of water, it can kill all the bacteria in four *gallons* of water every minute (one liter every four seconds). So far, Gadgil's invention has been used in places such as Brazil, Mexico, and the Philippines.

Cellophane

Unhealthy bacteria were once a serious problem in food, too. Keeping bacteria away sounds like an obvious solution, but that's not why a chemist named Jacques Edwin Brandenberger invented cellophane. In a restaurant in France in 1900, Brandenberger had the idea to coat tablecloths so that spills wouldn't cause stains. He tinkered with chemicals for eight years, but the best he could come up with was a layer of clear film that made the tablecloth too stiff to be useful. Brandenberger noticed that the chemical sheet peeled off the tablecloth easily, and that's when he realized he had invented a new kind of packaging.

Soon cellophane was very popular, but an important new feature was added in 1927, when William Hale Charch, an industrial scientist, figured out how to make cellophane waterproof. Because bacteria couldn't get through the clear wrapping, cellophane was an important aid to food safety.

Another twist in the story of cellophane occurred in 1930 when Richard Drew, an engineer in Minnesota, added a layer of sticky adhesive to one side of a long, narrow ribbon of cellophane and rolled it up. This was the beginning of the invention of Scotch tape. However, most of the Scotch tape used today was the result of yet another improvement made in 1961 by the

William Hale Charch was an inventor who figured out how to make cellophane waterproof.

same company that employed Drew. The improvement was to make the cellophane layer more flexible and so clear that when you stick it on something, it becomes nearly invisible. Today, adhesive tape can be found in every home.

The Microwave Oven

The most famous invention story of all concerns the microwave oven. A radio engineer named Percy Spencer was working in a laboratory with a device called a **magnetron**. A magnetron is built from a strong magnet, shaped so electricity passing through the magnet will create powerful radio waves. No energy is created or destroyed, but the energy carried by the electricity is changed into radio energy and emitted from the magnetron.

SLICED BREAD

You can still buy a loaf of unsliced bread from a bakery today, if you prefer to slice it yourself at home. However, once the electric toaster was invented in 1905, unevenly cut slices meant that toast often had burned spots. So Otto Frederick Rohwedder started working on a machine to cut bread into uniform slices, and he perfected it in 1928. At first, bakers told him no one would want presliced bread because it would go stale quickly. But with newly invented cellophane bags available, even sliced bread could stay fresh. This is an example of how the combined effects of different inventions can cause a big change.

One day in 1946, Spencer had a chocolate bar in his pocket when he happened to stand in front of a powerful magnetron. He noticed that the chocolate bar melted! His conclusion was that the radio waves had transferred heat energy to the chocolate bar. This was a legendary case of **serendipity**, which means discovering something while you are looking for something completely different. Spencer immediately developed the Radarange. This first microwave oven used a magnetron tuned to emit radio

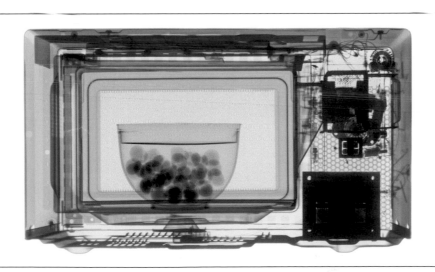

A modern microwave oven has been photographed to show the electronic control system and the magnetron inside.

waves that were very efficient at transferring energy to the chemicals in most foods. However, the machine was the size of a closet and weighed as much as a load of patio bricks! Like air-conditioning, it took more than ten years before microwave ovens were small enough for home use. Today, there are hundreds of millions of them.

Yet, despite all the improvements, you still can't make toast in the microwave. The microwave energy doesn't stop at the surface of any piece of food, so the entire slice of bread heats up, which prevents the chemical reaction that toasts the bread. Instead, the bread gets soggy in some places and hard in others, depending on how much microwave energy is absorbed in each part of the bread.

CHAPTER THREE

Power

In any of its various forms, energy is something that can accumulate: If you wait long enough, you can collect or use as much energy as you want. That's why another important idea is power, which tells how quickly energy is gathered or changed from one kind to another. A small candle left burning for a few hours might give off the same total energy as a light bulb does in just a few seconds, so we say the light bulb is more powerful than the candle.

A famous rule about energy is that it cannot be created or destroyed. So, when you use energy, as in a microwave oven or a toaster in your home, that energy has to come from somewhere and go somewhere else. Most of the energy you see around you has come from the Sun and traveled across 93 million miles (150 million km) of space to reach Earth. When you eat food, you are accessing energy that green plants stored when they absorbed sunlight. Coal and natural gas are examples of **fossil fuels**. Burning them is also a way of releasing energy that plants and microscopic animals took millions of years to store. When rain falls, the energy of its motion comes from sunlight, which causes water to evaporate from the surface of the ocean. All downhill motion of water comes from that energy.

The North American electric power distribution system includes thousands of transformer stations such as this one.

Enormous systems were built in the twentieth century to get the energy to you and make it convenient for you to use. The most efficient way of moving the energy across the landscape is through electricity. Scientists and engineers have an astonishing variety of schemes to generate and to transfer electricity. A generating station converts available energy into electricity and feeds it into the distribution system. In North America, enormous facilities to harness moving water and generate **hydroelectricity** were built on rivers such as the Niagara, the Columbia, and the Colorado. Coal-burning power stations were built in many cities as well. Are there power lines near your school? There is probably a generating station nearby.

Nuclear Energy

Albert Einstein, the most famous scientist of the twentieth century, discovered a whole new source of energy and power. In 1905, Einstein saw the connection between matter and energy, the two central ideas in physics. Natural radioactivity is an example of energy that comes directly from matter. Radioactivity occurs when something happens to the nucleus of an atom. For instance, the nucleus of a uranium atom can split into two smaller nuclei. This process is called **fission.**

POWER BLACKOUTS

Because electricity networks are so widespread and complex, there is always a risk that a problem can spread far from where it started. Severe weather, for instance, can knock out a power line and plunge an entire city into darkness for days. Even magnetic storms on the Sun have triggered trouble in places such as Quebec, Canada, where long power lines pick up such electrical disturbances. But the most famous power blackout of the twentieth century occurred on November 9, 1965, when the failure of a single fuse at a generating station near Niagara Falls left millions of people in big cities such as Boston and New York without electricity overnight or even longer.

A nuclear device called Owens was detonated at a test site in the Nevada desert in 1957.

When the nucleus splits, two nuclear particles called **neutrons** come rushing out. In 1932, a physicist named Leo Szilard realized that a neutron emitted from one uranium nucleus can hit another uranium nucleus and cause the second to split as well. This means that a **chain reaction** can occur from one nucleus to the next. Because two neutrons are released in each fission, the break-up of each uranium nucleus can result in the break-up of two other uranium nuclei. Thus, the chain reaction expands. Because this can happen very quickly, Szilard imagined that a tremendous amount of energy could be produced in a split second, making a very powerful bomb. Szilard even got a patent for the concept of such a bomb. Through the colossal efforts of many scientists in the United States during World War II, the first nuclear weapon was exploded in a test on July 16, 1945, in the New Mexico desert. This was the beginning of an age of frightening power.

In contrast to the horror of such a destructive weapon, scientists also knew that fission energy could be made to generate electricity. Szilard came up with the idea that the neutrons spilling out from one uranium nucleus to the next could be controlled if the generator had bricks made of carbon built into it. Precisely the right design would be needed, but a reactor like this could produce incredible heat. The first nuclear reactor was built under a stadium at the University of Chicago by Szilard's friend Enrico Fermi. This is where the first controlled chain reaction took place on December 2, 1942, even before the bomb project was complete.

After the war ended, developments in nuclear power took place in the United States, Britain, and Canada. All three countries soon had working nuclear reactors. On December 20, 1951, the first light bulbs powered by a nuclear reactor came on in a remote corner of southeastern Idaho. It was the Experimental Breeder Reactor, or EBR, located at the Idaho National Engineering Laboratory.

Heat from the uranium fuel turned water into steam, which drove a turbine not very different from the turbines that are found in hydroelectric or fossil-fuel powered facilities. All of these produce electricity by making a shaft turn inside a strong magnet. However, nuclear energy is one of only a few sources of power that do not come from the Sun: uranium fuel is mined from underground and has been there almost 5 billion years.

Giant turbines such as this one, driven by steam from a nuclear reactor or another source of energy, are at the heart of most generating stations.

Alkaline Batteries

Although batteries were available two hundred years ago, they required hazardous chemicals like acids. Chemicals that are not acids are called alkaline, and it was the renowned inventor Thomas Edison, who in 1903 developed the first alkaline battery.

Another inventor, a Canadian named Lew Urry, came up with an even better alkaline battery in 1959. The chemicals used in Urry's invention were powdered zinc, manganese dioxide, and carbon. His battery was smaller than Edison's but more powerful than other batteries available in the 1950s.

Urry took two toy cars and put his new battery in one and another popular battery in the other. Then, he turned the toy cars loose in the cafeteria of the factory where he worked. Everyone in the cafeteria cheered when one of the toy cars stopped, but Urry's battery had enough energy to carry the other toy all the way across the room. In 1980, the manufacturer of Urry's battery changed its name to Energizer. Batteries are probably the most versatile inventions of the twentieth century. You probably have a dozen of them in your own home.

ELECTRIC GENIUS

The method that is still used today to transmit electrical power over transmission wires, called "three-phase alternating current," was devised by Nikola Tesla. As an inventor in the late nineteenth century, Tesla was almost as famous as Thomas Edison. But while Edison turned his inventions into a successful business, Tesla became more and more eccentric over the years. He experimented with wireless signals and shared some of the credit for inventing radio with Guglielmo Marconi. Others projects included power turbines, focused lightning, gravity, and listening for messages from Mars! Scientists have concluded that many of his suggestions were impossible, but no one doubts that Tesla was an amazing genius.

Nikola Tesla calmly reads in his laboratory while artificial lightning forks above.

CHAPTER FOUR

Factories

All the amazing products we use every day come from somewhere, and most of them are put together in a factory. Instead of making things one at a time, a factory is a place where many products are made in a process. Every step in the process is thought out carefully so that many items can be made as quickly as possible. The use of energy and raw materials in the factory is monitored by experts. If they can think of a way to produce just as many products with less energy or fewer raw materials, that will make the process more efficient. Factories produce everything from tiny electronic parts to gigantic earth-moving machines. There are small factories with fewer than a dozen workers and enormous factories that employ thousands of people.

Assembly Lines

More than 200 years ago, factories in the United States developed the idea of specializing. Some workers were trained only to make certain parts, while other workers learned to make other parts. Then, the various parts were all put together by still other workers, who were trained only to do the assembly. This became known as "American-style" manufacturing. The Cadillac auto-

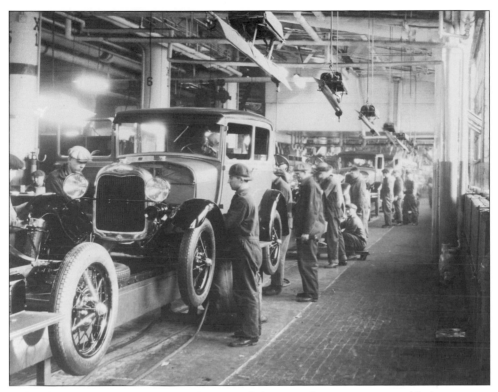

Workers bring large pieces of automobiles together on an assembly line at one of the Ford factories in 1913.

mobiles that impressed Frederick Bennet in 1908 came from this kind of factory. The twentieth century was dominated by specialized factories.

However, in the early American-style factories, workers would carry their work from one station in the factory to the next. They wasted a lot of time moving back and forth, and obviously this was not practical if the products were large and heavy. So Henry Ford built the first moving assembly line. He came up with the idea when he visited a meat-processing plant in 1912, where he saw animal carcasses hooked to an overhead rail. Each butcher sliced a particular cut of meat and gave the carcass a push so it would slide to the next butcher.

Ford was a businessman who already owned a factory in Detroit that manufactured an automobile called the Model T. He adopted the system used in the meat-processing plant. Large parts would move through the factory on a conveyor belt. Each worker would stay at his own station, doing the same thing to each part as it rolled by. Using the assembly-line technique, millions and millions of Model T cars were produced. Ford's goal was to sell the car at a price that even the factory workers themselves could afford. Before then, cars were so expensive that only rich people could buy them. At a lower price, more people could afford them, and many more cars would be sold. Based on this principle, the Ford Motor Company became one of the largest and most successful companies in history, and assembly-line manufacturing became one of the signatures of the century.

Toyota Production System

However, new problems came along with the improvements. Products such as automobiles are extremely complicated. Workers who contribute to only one tiny part lose interest in the whole product. They feel insignificant and don't work as hard as they could. That's why improvements to the management of factories have been just as important as improvements to the technology. At the end of World War II in Japan, two engineers, Shigeo Shingo and Taichii Ohno, devised some new ideas at a factory that made

THE GREAT SCREWDRIVER DEBATE

The sad thing about screws is that the original idea for how to drive them doesn't work very well. This is because slotted screwdrivers tend to slip out of a slotted screw. Two different inventors came up with solutions in the twentieth century. Peter Robertson was a salesman who, in 1908, thought up a design based on a square recess in the head of the screw, instead of a slot. The square screwdriver pushes on four edges and doesn't slip out. Then in 1936, Henry Phillips decided to try a recess shaped like a plus sign (+) to solve the problem of the slotted screw. People who work with tools have never stopped arguing about which is better!

Technicians work on a racing car in a modern Toyota factory.

Toyota automobiles. They got the workers involved by setting up small groups. Members would learn all the jobs of the others in their group. They would help each other and offer suggestions about how to make the process better. They realized that team-work would help to take the drudgery out of factory work.

Another advantage in Shingo and Ohno's system was how the parts were brought to the assembly line. In a Ford factory, huge warehouses stored a large supply of parts so they were ready when needed. At the Toyota factory, warehouses weren't needed because the parts arrived at the factory just in time to be used on the assembly line. The system required careful attention to detail because the deliveries had to be perfectly coordinated. The result was another major step forward in efficiency. Most large or complex factories around the world started using this method, which became known as "Just in Time" manufacturing.

The First Robots

In 1920, a science fiction writer named Karel Capek wrote a play about machines that looked almost human and did all the work in the factories. Capek's mechanical humanoids were called ro-bots, and they replaced human workers. The play was a warning that factories would become dehumanized. Humans would lose their sense of accomplishment if the robots did all the work.

LEVITTOWN

William Levitt and his brother, Alfred, ran a construction company in the 1940s. They built houses using mass production techniques similar to Henry Ford's assembly line. The first major project they designed for average families was on Long Island, New York. It began in 1947, and, eventually, they built a total of 17,000 houses! The project was a new suburb all by itself, called Levittown. The Levitts' company developed many more suburban projects in other states. The result was not just a new trend in houses, but a whole new way of life. In the United States today, twice as many people live in suburbs as in the central cities.

A robotic machine can perform welding operations very precisely, as seen in this multiple exposure photograph.

However, it's not so easy for a machine to mimic the complex abilities of a human being. No one in the past century was able to build a robot that could do as many different tasks as a human. However, in 1954, an inventor named George Devol decided to focus on one simple task: picking up a part, moving it somewhere else, and putting it down exactly where it was needed. Devol built a mechanical arm that could do this perfectly. Called the Unimate, it was expensive to build, but once it was installed, it could do the same step over and over again, all day long, without taking a rest. Industrial robots that could do dangerous or heavy jobs such as welding or painting were built in the 1970s. Although fewer human workers are required in factories today, robots have not completely replaced people.

Plastics

Leo Baekeland was a chemist who made a fortune by developing a formula for photographic paper. In 1904, Baekeland built a barn outside his mansion near New York City. He started to

Modern plastic juice containers are safe and inexpensive. Here, they are being filled in a food-processing plant.

experiment with gooey chemicals called **resins**. There are many resins in nature, such as sap from trees and the secretions of some insects. They can be stored in liquid form and then spread on like paint. Once natural resins harden, they become very useful protective coatings. However, natural resins were expensive because they were hard to collect and needed to be carefully refined. Baekeland wanted to invent an artificial resin that could be produced in a factory.

A few years later he did it: By mixing chemicals and heating them in a sealed container, he made a resin that could be heated and molded into any shape imaginable. Once the artificial resin was set hard, it was very strong and could not be damaged by heat or most chemicals. Also, his new resin was very good at insulating electrical energy. Power systems needed a product that could be used to mount or to hang wires carrying dangerous high-voltage electricity. The official chemical name of his invention was **polyoxybenzylmethylenglycolanhydride**, but Baekeland called it Bakelite, a name formed from his own. Bakelite was the first successful plastic.

CHAPTER FIVE

✈

In the Air

From a windswept beach in North Carolina late in 1903, Orville and Wilbur Wright took off into history. They owned a successful bicycle shop, but their real passion was for flying. They had spent a few years learning about **gliders**, making over a thousand flights without an engine. Then, the Wright brothers were ready to compete with other inventors around the world. The challenge: to build a heavier-than-air flying machine. It would have to take off from the ground under its own **power**, fly under the control of its pilot, and land safely.

Their first airplane was called the *Flyer*. The reason the Wright brothers succeeded was that they were already experienced glider pilots and skilled mechanics. They knew what was needed and how to build it. They invented a method of controlling the airplane in flight by twisting the wings. Cables were attached to the wings and connected to levers next to the pilot. Also, they invented their own propeller design, which was better than any other propeller at the time. They were the first flyers who understood that a propeller works on the same principle as a wing. A propeller pulls an airplane forward just as wings pull it upward. Finally, they built an engine specially intended for the *Flyer*. It was powerful enough to turn the two propellers at the correct

A historic moment during the Wright brothers' first flight at Kitty Hawk, North Carolina, in 1903.

speed, but light enough to sit safely onboard the plane. Everything came together for them when they made their take-off near the town of Kitty Hawk. They made four short but successful flights before the wind tipped over the *Flyer*. December 17 was the only day in 1903 that a human flew in an airplane.

Of course, there's a lot more to flying than heavier-than-air machines. Besides, gliders, parachutes, and hot-air balloons had been airborne for a hundred years already, and in 1900, there was the curious story of an airship in Germany. It was due to the enthusiasm of Count Ferdinand von Zeppelin, a former army officer. Zeppelin financed the construction of the *LZ-1*. Built on a floating dock in a lake, *LZ-1* was more than 400 feet (120 m) long. When the Wright brothers flew their heavier-than-air machine a few years later, the total length of its first flight was less than a third the length of the *LZ-1*!

Dirigibles

The *LZ-1* was an example of a rigid airship. They are also called **dirigibles** or even **Zeppelins**, after the count himself. They had a thin skeleton made of metal. Large airtight bags were nestled within the wiry framework. A cabin for crew, cargo, or passengers was built along the bottom of the Zeppelin. When the bags were filled with a gas that is lighter than air, the huge airship lifted majestically off the ground. Like hot-air balloons and nonrigid blimps, Zeppelins float rather than fly. They work on the principle of buoyancy, which is a force that pushes upward on anything that is less dense overall than air. It is the same principle that holds a ship up on the surface of the water. The lighter-than-air gas that was used in those days was hydrogen.

There were three successful flights of the *LZ-1* in 1900, but no other investors were interested, and the whole idea stalled for a few years. Meanwhile, heavier-than-air machines were immediately popular, and many inventors added improvements in just a few years. The main advantage airplanes had over airships was that they were easier to control in windy conditions. By the 1930s, both Zeppelins and airplanes were in service around the world, carrying passengers and cargo. However, a Zeppelin called the *Hindenburg* was destroyed in a fiery crash in New

AIRPORTS

Soon after the Wright brothers demonstrated their flying machine, there were planes flying everywhere, but to get back on the ground safely, an airplane needs a smooth place where it can roll for hundreds of feet (or meters) and stop after touching down. There were many places where support services such as fuel supplies and hangars were located near a runway during the 1910s. A specialized landing field was first called an airport in 1919. Grooved pavement was invented for airports so that water would run off a landing strip instead of making an airplane skid when it landed. By the end of the twentieth century, there were almost 10,000 airports registered around the world.

Huge Zeppelins, such as the LZ-2, took to the air in the early decades of the twentieth century.

Jersey in 1937, and this ruined the reputation of Zeppelins. Part of the reason why the *Hindenburg* disaster was so famous is that the hydrogen in the Zeppelin burned ferociously when it ignited. Today, lighter-than-air vessels are filled with nonflammable helium, but they may never again be as popular as airplanes.

Jet Engines

A major improvement for airplanes was the development and use of jet engines instead of propellers. In the late 1920s, Frank Whittle, an engineer in Britain, brought together basic ideas about the design of jet engines. Whittle also took flying lessons with the Royal Air Force. He was convinced that jet propulsion could help airplanes fly at faster speeds and higher altitudes.

There was also an engineer in Germany named Hans von Ohain who was thinking about the same solution for improving airplane performance. Ohain received government support in Germany before Whittle did in Britain. Because of World War II,

Most fighter aircraft in World War II were moved forward through the air by propellers and did not have swept-back wings.

both countries began testing right away. They both wanted to build jet aircraft as soon as possible. However, by the time the first jet fighters flew, the war was almost over. Afterward, Ohain and Whittle became good friends and helped each other promote the new technology.

Although a jet engine has small blades that resemble propellers, the blades are used to compress the air coming into the engine, not to drive the plane forward as a propeller does. Instead, the compressed air is mixed with high-energy fuel and ignited. When the fuel burns, it expands with tremendous power. Because the jet engine is built so that the expanded fuel mixture can only exit out the back, there is a very powerful forward thrust. The exhaust is going extremely fast, which is why jet aircraft are capable of such incredible speed. Propeller-driven airplanes can't compete because a propeller doesn't push air backward as fast as a jet engine can.

Swept-Back Wings

The most obvious feature of an airplane is its wings. For the first few decades of flight, wings were designed to extend straight out from the body of the airplane at a 90-degree angle. Today, that style is seen only on low-speed or smaller airplanes. The reason is that a wing like that has problems that start at higher speeds, so early slow-flying airplanes weren't affected.

The study of forces and movements in flight is called **aerodynamics**. It is a very complicated subject and involves some of the most advanced mathematical formulas ever devised. Even some experts who have a good feel for flying don't try to understand the equations, but one way to visualize what makes a plane stay in the air is to imagine following the molecules of air as they rush over the body and wings of the airplane. When you think of a plane with the original-style of wings, you can see that the onrushing air hits the front of the wing all at once. The resulting shock is dangerous for the wing, and the danger increases as the airplane goes faster.

A German aerodynamics expert hit upon a solution in the years before World War II. His name was Adolph Busemann. He realized that if the wing was attached to the airplane at a different angle instead of 90 degrees, each molecule of air would hit the front of the wing at a different time. The air that was closest

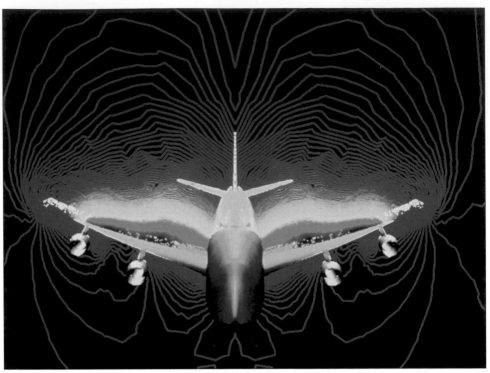

A computer-generated image shows the low pressure zones (yellow) on top of the wings of a large, modern passenger jet aircraft.

to the airplane's body would hit the wing first, and the farther away a molecule was from the body, the later it would hit the wing. Thus, the air could flow over the wing more smoothly. This design became known as the swept-back wing. When Busemann first presented his invention in 1935, no airplane had been built that flew fast enough to need swept-back wings, but German designers kept the idea in mind, and some of the fastest planes they built before the end of World War II had swept-back wings. Today, with routine airline flights traveling nearly at the speed of sound, almost every large, fast airplane has this feature.

Rockets

When chemicals burn very quickly, they push on everything around them. It was a thousand years ago that chemists in China discovered how to make gunpowder. One application for gunpowder was to pack it into a small cylinder that had an opening in one end, called a **nozzle**. When the gunpowder was lit, the expanding gases were expelled out the nozzle and caused a force that pushed the rocket high into the air. Rockets were often used both as weapons and as fireworks.

A rocket carries with it all the chemicals it needs, whereas a jet engine or even an automobile motor must draw in air to mix with the fuel. This is a big advantage for jets in the atmosphere. Because there is no air in space, rockets have the advantage there. Most of today's rockets use liquid chemicals held in tanks, with complicated plumbing to feed the chemicals to the nozzle where the combustion of the fuel takes place.

It was Robert Goddard who invented the liquid-fuel rocket. It was launched on March 16, 1926, near Auburn, Massachusetts. Its flight lasted a mere 2.5 seconds and rose only 41 feet (14 m)

Robert H. Goddard (*second from left*) poses with one of the liquid-fuelled rockets he developed in New Mexico.

above a cold farmer's field, but we could say that the rocket was aimed straight at the stars. Goddard later moved to the wide-open spaces of New Mexico and continued to improve his designs.

Although rockets are most famous for launching spaceships beyond Earth's atmosphere, many high-speed airplanes have been powered by rockets. One very famous rocket-powered

THE MOON LANDING

No event in the twentieth century involved more inventions than the U.S. space program that first landed humans on the Moon in July of 1969. For instance, a tiny quartz crystal to control an electronic clock helped keep the weight and power requirements of the Apollo spacecraft to a minimum. Cordless power tools such as drills resulted from the need for astronauts on the Moon to drill into the rocks there, far from any place to plug in. Even the food eaten by the astronauts involved an invention you might have eaten yourself—freeze-dried food in packages. Joy sticks, just like the one you might use with a computer game, were first developed for spacecraft controls.

Apollo 15 Commander David R. Scott gives a military salute to the U.S. flag during a 1971 moonwalk.

Satellites, such as this one in outer space, use a large dish antenna to send and receive signals.

flight on October 14, 1947, made Chuck Yeager, a U.S. Air Force test pilot, the first human to fly faster than the speed of sound. The *X-15*, which took pilots high enough to be right on the edge of outer space, was another well-known rocket plane. For sheer excitement, it's hard to top a rocket.

Communications Satellites

Every invention starts with a simple thought, something that has never occurred to anyone else before. Then, the idea has to be turned into something practical. One day in the 1940s, Arthur C. Clarke was thinking about spaceships in orbit around Earth. An orbit is a path in outer space around the globe. The speed that a satellite travels in its orbit is determined by how far above the ground it is.

Clarke knew that a satellite in a circular orbit 22,300 miles (36,000 km) above Earth will travel at just the right speed to go around in exactly 24 hours. So, if the orbit is aligned with the equator, it will seem to hover motionless above a particular spot as Earth turns underneath, also in 24 hours. The satellite would be **geostationary**, meaning standing over Earth.

Clarke was a British radio engineer, and he understood how useful it would be for radio signals to be relayed from a transmitter to a receiver far away. He realized that a geostationary orbit would be a perfect place for such a relay. A transmitter could be aimed and locked onto a relay satellite. The relayed signal could be received by antennas over a very wide area on the ground, almost a third of the entire world. It took almost twenty years until the first communications satellites were launched, but today such an orbit is called a Clarke orbit.

CHAPTER SIX

Medicine

Whats going on inside the human body? When someone gets sick, you want to know what the specific problem is right away. However, it is also important to learn the general scientific principles of how the body works. Doctors in the twentieth century had incredible new technological triumphs to help them probe the body.

Medical Imaging

The simplest thing a doctor can do is look, touch, and listen to the body from the outside. Yet, the view inside gives much more detail. After **X-rays** were discovered, just before the beginning of the twentieth century, they were used extensively both to figure out what was wrong with patients and to study how the body works. This is still the most common type of medical imaging today.

X-rays are a form of **electromagnetic radiation**. Ordinary light and all radio transmissions are different examples of the same thing. All of these travel through space or matter and come in little packets, or bursts, called photons. Three characteristics distinguish one kind of photon from another: wavelength, frequency, and energy, but these three characteristics are all different aspects of the same thing, so most scientists only talk about the energy of electromagnetic radiation. Photons of radio trans-

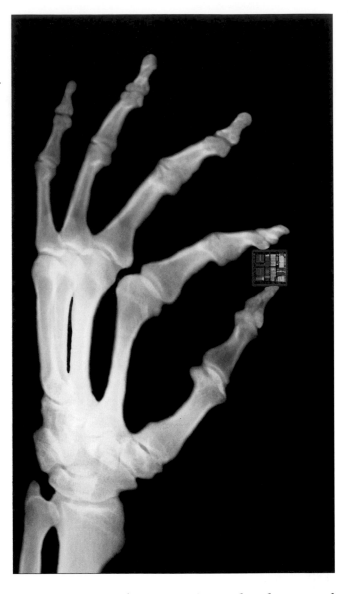

An X-ray image of a healthy human hand holding a microchip shows the bones clearly because the X-rays pass through the skin and muscles but not through the bone.

missions carry the lowest amount of energy. A single photon of ordinary light carries at least a thousand times as much as a photon of radio transmission, but an X-ray photon carries a million times more than that. Even though the total amount of energy is still fairly small, an X-ray photon has enough punch to pass at least partly through skin and bones.

A medical X-ray machine begins with a source of X-rays that is aimed at part of the patient's body. The X-rays that make it through are then captured on specially formulated film or an electronic detector that is positioned on the other side of the patient. Sometimes a special chemical is placed in a particular part of the body to block the X-rays aimed at that spot. In shadowy likeness, the picture shows the target in incredibly fine detail. A recent invention in X-ray technology, called computerized tomography, actually provides a three-dimensional look inside the body. To an expert eye, all kinds of medical problems become obvious right away.

Ultrasound

However, X-rays are themselves hazardous, so patients should not have too many of them. In 1953, a heart specialist and a physics student were thinking about the shortcomings of X-rays. X-rays

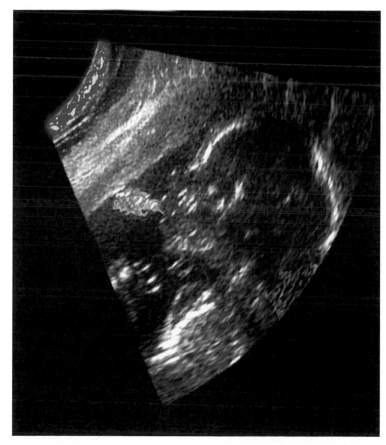

An ultrasound picture of a fetus inside a mother's body shows its head to be the large shape in the middle.

work best with still pictures. An X-ray picture of an organ that moves rapidly, such as the heart, doesn't give a doctor enough information to determine what might be wrong. Inge Edler, the doctor, and Carl Hellmuth Hertz, the student, worked at a university in Sweden. Edler asked Hertz if he thought something like radar would do the job, bouncing a radio wave off the target instead of passing through. Hertz had been using high-frequency sound waves, called **ultrasound**, to probe solid objects in his laboratory. Reflected sound waves had already been used underwater to detect icebergs. Other doctors had tried to use ultrasound to check the brain and the gallbladder. Edler and Hertz decided to try aiming ultrasound through the chest of a person.

On October 29, 1953, they managed to get the first echoes from a beating heart. By analyzing the echoes, Edler was able to distinguish if a certain valve in the heart was functioning properly. After numerous improvements, ultrasound machines became common in clinics and hospitals everywhere. The equipment is not as expensive as many other medical machines. Perhaps the technique is most famous for showing a human fetus before birth. Ask your parents if they saw an ultrasound of you before you were born.

HUMAN TRANSPLANTS

A hundred years ago, an eye doctor in Europe named Eduard Konrad Zirm knew that doctors had tried many times to replace the protective front layer of the eye, called the cornea, but none had ever succeeded. In 1905, there was a tragic coincidence between two patients whose eyes were hurt. An 11-year-old boy was hit by metal splinters, which damaged his eye but nevertheless left his corneas in good condition. Meanwhile, an adult worker was blinded by a chemical spill. Zirm transplanted the young person's corneas into the man's eyes and restored the man's vision. Eventually, doctors learned how to transplant many other human organs, including the liver, the lungs, and even the heart.

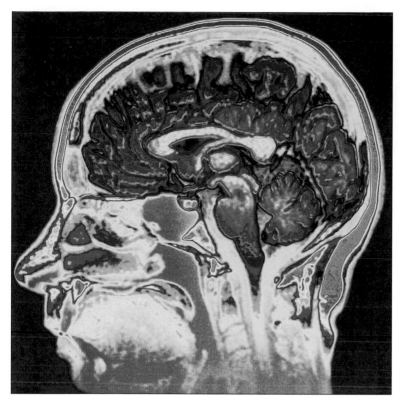

By analyzing the data from an MRI scan, doctors can generate a side view of a person's head and see a picture of the brain inside.

MRI

In addition to X-rays and ultrasound, scientists have developed an imaging technique based on magnetism. It is called **MRI**, which stands for magnetic resonance imaging. MRI is a complicated and expensive process. One advantage is that it doesn't send any hazardous radiation into the body. Instead, a powerful electric magnet is lined up with the part of the body that the doctors want to look at. The magnets used by MRI machines are enormous, and some are cooled with liquid helium. Inside the cells of the body, individual atoms of hydrogen are forced to line up with the magnet. Then, a small burst of radio waves is sent across the body, and the lined-up hydrogen atoms turn into extremely tiny radio relays, transmitting the energy back in a predictable way. The MRI machine detects these transmissions. As with X-rays and ultrasound, the information is analyzed and interpreted by the doctors.

Penicillin

Many wonder drugs were invented in the twentieth century, such as salvarsan, insulin, cyclosporine, and more. However, the most curious story concerns Alexander Fleming, the physician who discovered **penicillin**. In 1928, Fleming left some small plates on a bench in his laboratory in England. He was studying bacteria, so there were bacteria on those small plates. Perhaps if the plates had been properly cleaned, the discovery would never have happened.

Fleming went away for a few days of vacation. When he returned, he looked at the bacteria on the plates. After so many hours, there should have been plenty of growing bacteria visible. However, Fleming noticed something peculiar: There were patches among the bacteria where none was growing. Knowing that the air everywhere is filled with mold spores all the time, Fleming figured that some spores had fallen on the plates. Fleming realized there must be a type of mold that could prevent the bacteria from growing.

Like every good scientist, Fleming wrote a report about his discovery. However, he was not able to separate out the mold that stopped the bacteria and soon gave up on the project. In addi-

DDT

Not all inventions remain successful forever. DDT is a specialized chemical that was first invented in the nineteenth century. Then in 1939, a Swiss chemist named Paul Hermann Müller discovered that DDT has the power to kill mosquitoes and other insect pests. Health agencies around the world used huge amounts of DDT to control these pests through the 1950s. In a famous book called *Silent Spring*, author Rachel Carson put forward the idea that DDT also harmed birds. The book influenced people to ban DDT and inspired people everywhere to be concerned about nature and the environment. By the end of the twentieth century, it was unthinkable that a powerful chemical like DDT would ever be widely used again.

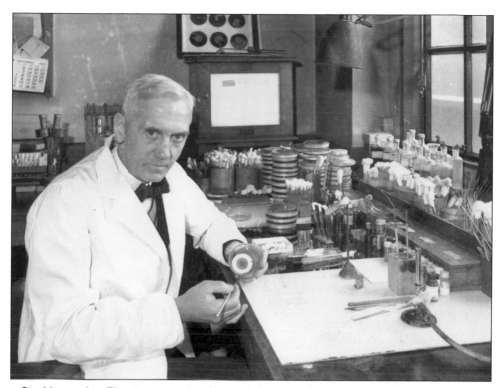

Sir Alexander Fleming was the Scottish bacteriologist who discovered penicillin in 1928.

tion to Fleming, there were many other medical experts looking for new ideas in the battle against bacteria. In 1938, Ernst Chain saw the report Fleming had written. Chain found the right mold and went to work, but he and his team also struggled to determine how Fleming's mold spore could halt the growth of bacteria. Eventually, they succeeded while World War II was raging around them. The need to help wounded soldiers was great, so penicillin was in tremendous demand.

Penicillin was not easy to manufacture. It was the late 1940s before drug companies were able to provide enough penicillin to help everyone who needed it. Not only did it help the human body's natural defense against bacteria, but it had no unhealthy side effects of its own. Millions of people have been saved from infection by penicillin over the years.

CHAPTER SEVEN

>-+-

Information

E arly computers were really just mechanical calculators. They used turning shafts and gears to perform routine arithmetic. Numbers were represented by the position of the shafts and gears. Even a person skilled in the use of an ancient invention called the abacus could compete with a mechanical calculator. Mechanical calculators were already common in the first fifty years of the twentieth century. Many of them were driven by motors that used electricity as their source of energy.

Still, no one thought of using variations in electricity to represent numbers instead of to power a mechanical device. By the 1930s, some telephone systems used automatic electric switches to connect phone lines for making calls. A telephone call transferred information by human voice, but the electric device that did the connecting was not a computer. Nevertheless, it was devices such as these that got Claude Shannon thinking about electricity. Shannon was a university student from Michigan who studied both electrical engineering and mathematics. This was the perfect combination for the founding father of the electronic communications age and the advent of the computer and telecommunications industries.

Shannon realized that the switching of phone lines could be represented by purely mathematical concepts. He also saw that all mathematical functions, beginning with the simple ones such as addition and multiplication, could be performed by electronic switches. The switches would cause variations in electricity—pulses—to be sent through the circuitry. These pulses could represent anything: numbers, letters, symbols. A key advantage is that the pulses didn't have to be measured, just counted. This avoided the inaccuracy of trying to measure electricity as it whizzed by. The word **digital** refers to something based on counting, instead of measuring.

When he went on to continue his studies at the Massachusetts Institute of Technology, Shannon wrote an article in 1937. In the article, he explained how the principles of digital logic could be applied to circuitry. To emphasize that the electricity was being controlled as information instead of being used to transfer energy, a new word was coined: **electronics**. This launched a whole new world. Digital electronic computers were soon being designed and built at universities and government laboratories, both in the United States and in England. One example was the ENIAC (an acronym for Electronic Numerical Integrator and Computer), built by the U.S. Army during World War II to assist in the calculations required for aiming weapons.

MORSE CODE

After Samuel Morse invented the telegraph system in the nineteenth century, there was a scheme called Morse Code for translating letters and numbers into electric pulses. To shorten messages and speed up communication even more, specific combinations of letters were used for special situations. The idea of standardizing these code combinations, however, had to wait until an international conference in Berlin, Germany, in 1906. A famous example of the new code words was a call for help: three short pulses, followed by three long pulses and then three more short pulses. In Morse Code, this spells out SOS. The new distress call was used for the first time by the luxury liner RMS *Titanic*, which sank in the north Atlantic on April 15, 1912.

Operators make adjustments to ENIAC, one of the first electronic computers in the 1940s. The computer covered the entire wall of the room.

The Stored-Program Concept

It wasn't easy to program the first computers, however. They
were giant devices as big as an entire room. For ENIAC, program-
ming involved rerouting some of the wiring, which could take
many hours of work. John von Neumann changed all that. Von
Neumann was a brilliant mathematician from Hungary. In 1930,
he came to the United States to work at the famous Institute for
Advanced Study at Princeton University. During World War II,
von Neumann was part of the Manhattan Project, a colossal
effort to develop the first nuclear bomb. As the war was ending,
he wrote a report about one of the first digital electronic computers, EDVAC (which was an acronym for Electronic Discrete
Variable Automatic Computer). In this report, von Neumann
suggested that the program for the computer could be stored and
manipulated electronically. Like data, it could be changed, updated, or replaced easily, without pulling apart any of the computers's complicated circuitry. Today, we take it for granted that new
programs can be installed as easily as any other data.

Transistors and Chips

The reason those early computers were such hulks is that they used glass tubes with complicated wire grids in them to control the pulses. Then, in 1947, three scientists (William Shockley, John Bardeen, and Walter Brattain) working at a telephone company's research laboratory in New Jersey developed a solid crystal that did the same job as the glass tube and wire grids. The company decided to call this invention a **transistor**. It was inexpensive to manufacture and required only a tiny amount of

MOBILES

You might not expect that something as simple as a new kind of hanging decoration had to wait until the 1930s, but the inventor of mobiles was artist Alexander Calder. It was his radical idea to hang brightly colored shapes on curved wires of various lengths so that they would swing and turn on the slightest air movement. The most famous examples of Calder's mobiles are very large, such as the one hanging in the atrium at the National Gallery of Art in Washington. It is 76 feet (23 m) long and weighs 920 pounds (420 kg)! Mobiles that you might have in your own room work the same way, but are much smaller.

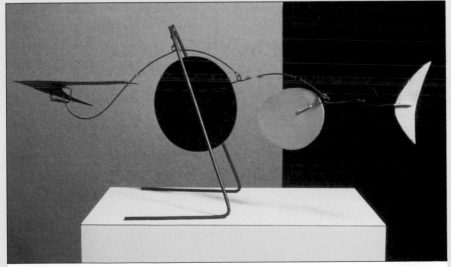

"Boomerange and Sickle Moon" is one of Alexander Calder's mobiles.

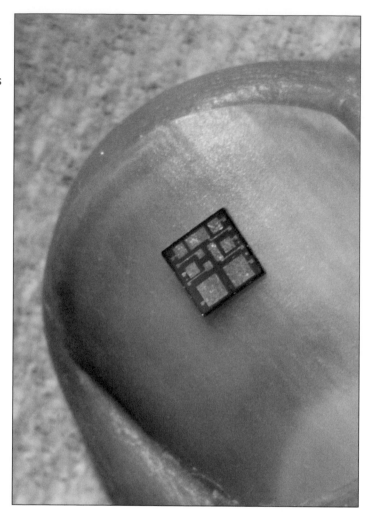

A microchip such as this one, perched on a person's fingernail, has far more computing power than early computers such as ENIAC.

electricity to make it work. Computers made of transistors could be crammed into much smaller packages.

The transistor had an even greater advantage. Its basic principle was that it could control pulses of electricity. The pulses in a digital computer didn't need to carry a lot of power, so a transistor didn't have to be large. Manufacturers developed techniques to build smaller and smaller transistors. Meanwhile, a British electronics engineer named Geoffrey Dummer came up with a radical idea in 1952: Why not build an entire **circuit** on one solid crystal? It was a tremendous idea, although Dummer wasn't actually able to build his invention. However, by the late 1950s, manufac-

turers in the United States did figure out how to make such minia-
ture circuits. Officially called **integrated circuits**, they became
known as "**chips**." Some were as small as your fingernail. In fact,
the technique improved so much that by the end of the century,
a single chip had millions of transistors on it.

The Internet
Thanks to integrated circuits, computers spread into homes,
offices, and factories throughout the world. The last great invention of the twentieth century links those computers together. It is
the Internet. A U.S. government agency devoted to advanced
research projects started its development in the early 1960s. The
original purpose was to find a way to transfer information among
computers in the event of a terrible catastrophe, such as war. It
was necessary for information to be sent and received by separate

In the 1920s, many young people used home made kits to listen to radio
signals transmitted from around the world.

computers, even if they were programmed using different mathematical codes. Basic rules, called **protocols**, were established so that any computer could formulate data that could be understood by other computers.

In 1971, Ray Tomlinson, one of the computer engineers working on the early Internet, was testing new ways of sending short messages from one computer to another. He invented the idea of using the @ symbol to separate the name of the person from the name of the computer host. This was the first e-mail message. Almost twenty years later, on August 6, 1991, a physicist named Tim Berners-Lee wrote a protocol that would allow a variety of files, such as pictures, to be offered to the Internet as links. A computer user with a mouse could click on a link and another file would be transferred from a host computer called a **server**. Berners-Lee called this invention the World Wide Web. Within a few years, there were millions of servers available to anyone.

Radio and Television

Before homes had computers, television sets were the coolest thing in high technology, and before that, there was radio. Both radio and television share a basic principle: Signals are sent from a transmitter to a receiver without any wires or other connections between them. The information is coded in **photons** of energy. These are similar to ordinary visible light, but with lower energy per photon.

Simple versions of radio had already been demonstrated by engineers such as Nikolai Tesla, Alexander Popov, and Guglielmo Marconi before 1900. In 1906, a Canadian electronics pioneer named Reginald Fessenden sent the first modern radio broadcast. He played the holiday song "O, Holy Night" on his violin and transmitted it to ships at sea.

Engineers knew right away that radio signals could be coded to carry the information needed to form a picture, but how could the picture be displayed? The answer was the cathode-ray tube, which had also been invented before 1900. It is a glass tube, flared at one end and coated with special chemicals that light up when electricity strikes them. When Philo Taylor Farnsworth was a high school student in a farming community in Idaho, he

Green laser light on a laboratory bench can be bounced off mirrors and then studied by instruments.

A young person born in the twentieth century uses a computer, which was invented in the twentieth century, but continues to be updated.

thought he could devise an electronic circuit that would aim a beam inside a cathode-ray tube. By controlling the beam, he reasoned it should cause a recognizable image to form. Farnsworth was finally ready to give a public demonstration of his invention in Philadelphia on August 25, 1934. This was the true birth of modern television.

Lasers

There are many ways to make something give off light. Heating the object to a few hundred degrees will make it glow a dull red, and if you could heat it to a few thousand degrees, it would give off a bright white light. Fluorescent tubes are another example. They work by sending electricity through a gas. The gas converts the electric power into **ultraviolet** light. The inside of a fluorescent tube is coated with a chemical, similar to the coating inside a cathode-ray tube. The coating absorbs the ultraviolet light and gives off a very pure white glow because photons are emitted when electrons flip from a higher to a lower energy level.

However, there is another way to make photons come out of a vast number of atoms. It's called **stimulated emission** and requires that the whole collection of atoms start off with their electrons pumped up to the same state of high energy. Then, sending a very weak beam of light at the proper energy will stimulate the electrons so that a significant fraction of them all give off matching photons. The original beam of light is amplified tremendously.

Charles Townes and Gordon Gould were the scientists who invented this process. Gould called it light amplification by stimulated emission of radiation, or laser for short. Laser technology improved rapidly. By 1974, the first supermarket scanners using lasers became available. Lasers are also a key component of modern compact disc players, which appeared in 1982 and DVD players, which came along just before the end of the century.

Glossary

aerodynamics – the study of forces and movements in flight

ammonia – a hazardous chemical (NH_2) used in air-conditioning equipment

bacteria – tiny living cells. There are thousands upon thousands of different types. Some are harmful, some are helpful. Billions of bacteria live inside your body, coexisting with your cells. Most of the time, this is not a problem.

CFCs – chlorofluorocarbons. Chemicals based on chlorine, fluorine, and carbon. Used in air-conditioning equipment and, formerly, in spray cans

chain reaction – a process in which neutrons from the fission of one atomic nucleus cause two or more other atomic nuclei to split apart, and so on

chip – see *integrated circuit*

circuit – a complete path for electricity to flow from source to destination and back

digital – related to counting, as opposed to measuring

dirigible – a rigid airship, with one or more large sealed bags of lighter-than-air gas held together in a frame. Also called a Zeppelin

electromagnetic radiation — a form of energy that travels in packets called photons, characterized by wavelength, frequency, and energy. There is a tremendous range of electromagnetic radiation. It travels through empty space at the speed of light.

electronics – the use of electricity as information, rather than to transfer energy

fission – the breakup of an atomic nucleus. A lot of energy can sometimes be released when fission occurs.

fossil fuels – coal, petroleum, natural gas, and other materials that are left underground by the decay of green plants and other living things. Fossil fuels are a valuable source of energy.

geostationary – an orbit that seems to stand still over Earth. Also called a Clarke orbit

glider – an airplane that is not powered

hydroelectricity – the generation of power from a turbine that is made to turn by flowing water, either from a fast-moving river or a waterfall

integrated circuit – a wafer-thin crystal with an electronic circuit composed of many transistors constructed on it

magnetron – a device that produces microwaves. It consists of a hollow magnet and a power source.

MRI – magnetic resonance imaging. A technique for probing the workings of the body that uses magnets to make hydrogen atoms in the body line up and emit electromagnetic radiation that can be scanned

neutron – an uncharged nuclear particle, about the same size as the positively charged proton

nozzle – the opening at the back of rocket where the hot combustion exhaust rushes out at very high speed

ozone – a molecule of oxygen (O_3) that has one more atom of oxygen than ordinary oxygen molecules. Ozone has a sharp, electric odor. Breathing ozone in large quantities would be dangerous. Near the surface of Earth, ozone is considered a type of pollution, but high in Earth's atmosphere, ozone is good because it absorbs cancer-causing ultraviolet light from the Sun.

penicillin – a drug that can prevent bacteria from multiplying; derived from mold spores

photon – the smallest individual piece of energy in electromagnetic radiation. The wavelength and frequency of a photon are other characteristics that can be measured or calculated.

polyoxybenzylmethylenglycolanhydride – the official chemical name of Bakelite, the first modern plastic

power – the rate at which energy is converted, transferred, or made available

protocols – in computer technology, rules that permit different types of computers to transfer data among themselves

resins – gooey chemicals that harden when they dry; often used as protective coatings

serendipity – finding something while you are looking for something completely different

server – a computer that makes files available over the Internet according to the protocols of the World Wide Web

stimulated emission – a process that emits light so that the photons are all strictly in step with each other

tar – a thick, gooey liquid often used to seal roofs or the wooden hulls of boats

tarmac or **tar macadam** – a mixture of tar and crushed slag from metal furnaces to spread on top of gravel roads

transistor – a single solid crystal that acts as a switch for pulses of electricity so the pulses can be counted as electronic information

ultrasound – high-frequency sound waves. Any vibrating object, like a stereo speaker or human vocal cords, produces sound waves. However, the human ear cannot hear ultrasound waves, which vibrate faster than about 20,000 times per second.

ultraviolet – photons of energy that have somewhat more energy than visible light, but not as much as X-rays

X-rays – extremely high energy photons

Zeppelin – see *dirigible*

Bibliography

"About: Inventors." About online. http://inventors.about.com

Absolute Astronomy online. www.absoluteastronomy.com/Reference.htm

Bloomfield, Louis. *How Things Work: The Physics of Everyday Life*. Hoboken, NJ: John Wiley & Sons, 2006.

Clarke, Donald. *The Encyclopedia of How It Works*. New York: A &W, 1977.

Davies, Eryl. *Inventions*. New York: Dorling Kindersley, 1995.

Global Future: Strategies for a Global Age online. www.globalfuture.com

"Greatest Engineering Achievements of the 20th Century." National Academy of Engineering online. www.greatachievements.org

The Great Idea Finder online. www.ideafinder.com

Hegedus, Alanna, and Rainey, Kaitlin. *Bleeps and Blips to Rocket Ships: Great Inventions in Communications*. Toronto: Tundra Books, 2001.

"The History of Air Conditioning." Carrier Corporation online. www.carrier.com.lb/history.htm

"How Electricity Travels to Your Home." Fusion Anomaly online. http://fusionanomaly.net/howelectricitytravelstoyourhome.html

"Invention and Discovery: Atomic Bombs and Fission." Nuclear Weapon Archive online. http://nuclearweaponarchive.org/Usa/Med/Discfiss.html

"A Look at the Beginnings of Windshields." Glasslinks online. www.glasslinks.com/newsinfo/early_ws.htm

"NASA Inventions in Everyday Life." NASA Solutions online. http://techtran.msfc.nasa.gov/classroom.html

Prelinger Archives online. www.archive.org/details.php?identifier=Pa2096Tacoma

Reid, Struan. *Invention & Discovery*. London: Usborne, 1986.

"A Short History Lesson on Plastic." SKS Bottle & Packaging, Inc. online. www.sks-bottle.com/Plastic_Bottle_History.html

Turvey, Peter. *Inventions, Inventors & Ingenious Ideas*. New York: Franklin Watts, 1992.

"Timeline of 20th Century Inventions." Maxfield & Montrose Interactive Inc. online. www.maxmon.com/timeline.htm

"The Top 100 Scientists and Thinkers of the 20th Century." The Time 100 online. www.time.com/time/time100/scientist

"Who Was the First to Fly?" Aerospace Web online. www.aerospaceweb.org/question/history/q0159.shtml

Williams, Trevor. *A History of Invention: From Stone Axes to Silicon Chips*. London: Time Warner Books, 2003.

"The Zamboni Story." Frank J. Zamboni & Co. Inc. online. www.zamboni.com/story/story.html

Further Exploration

BOOKS

Anderson, Maxine. *Amazing Leonardo da Vinci Inventions You Can Build Yourself.* Norwich, VT: Nomad Press, 2006.

Carlson, Laurie. *Thomas Edison for Kids: His Life and Ideas.* Chicago: Chicago Review Press, 2006.

Clements, Gillian. *The Picture History of Great Inventors.* London: Frances Lincoln, 2005.

Haskins, Jim. *Outward Dreams: Black Inventors and Their Inventions.* New York: Walker Books for Young Readers, 2003.

Landau, Elaine. *The History of Everyday Life.* Breckenridge, CO: Twenty-First Century Books, 2005.

Platt, Richard. *Eureka! Great Inventions and How They Happened.* Boston: Kingfisher, 2003.

Robinson, James. *Inventions.* Boston: Kingfisher, 2005.

Tomecek, Stephen M. *What a Great Idea! Inventions That Changed the World.* New York: Scholastic Nonfiction, 2003.

WEB SITES

www.bbc.co.uk/dna/h2g2/C468
This BBC site displays a list of inventions and the stories behind them.

www.exploravision.org/2005/what_is_exploravision.htm
The site profiles the Exploravision competition for young inventors.

www.invent.org/hall_of_fame/1_0_0_hall_of_fame.asp
The National Inventors Hall of Fame provides information about thousands of inventions and inventors.

www.littleexplorers.com/inventors
The site provides an online dictionary of inventions.

www.nsta.org/programs/craftsman/
The official site of the National Science Teachers Association's competition for young inventors provides information about past winning inventions created by young people.

web.mit.edu/invent
This is the official site for the Lemelson-MIT Program, which celebrates inventors who have turned their ideas into accomplishments.

Index

About the Author

PETER JEDICKE teaches mathematics and science at Fanshawe College in London, Canada. He has studied physics and philosophy, and is an active amateur astronomer, involved both locally and nationally in the Royal Astronomical Society of Canada. Jedicke has written articles for *Astronomy* magazine and *Sky & Telescope* magazine. His other books include *Cosmology: Exploring the Universe*, *SETI: The Search for Alien Intelligence,* and *Scientific American's The Big Idea.*

Picture Credits

PAGE 3: © Gunter Marx Photography/CORBIS
 8: © Getty Images
 9: © Barry Rowland/Age Foto Stock
11: © Bettmann/CORBIS
13: © Lester Lefkowitz/CORBIS
14: © Yang Liu/CORBIS
16: © Bernard Hoffman/Time Life Pictures/Getty Images
18: © William Taufic/CORBIS
20: © Keystone/Getty Images
21: © Gusto/Photo Researchers, Inc.
24: © Chris Knapton/Photo Researchers, Inc.
26: © US Department of Energy/Photo Researchers, Inc.
28: © Steve Allen/Photo Researchers Inc.
29: © Bettmann/CORBIS
31: © Getty Images
33: © Stuart Franklin/Getty Images
35: © D. Parker/Photo Researchers, Inc.
36: © Philippe Psaila/Photo Researchers, Inc
39: © Science Source
41: © Time Life Pictures/Mansell/Time Life Pictures/Getty Images
42: © Horace Bristol/CORBIS
44: © NASA/Science Source
45: © Hulton Archive/Getty Images
46: © CORBIS
47: © Imtek Imagineering, Inc./CORBIS
50: © Charles O'Rear/CORBIS
51: © Neil Borden/Photo Researchers, Inc.
53: © Pete Saloutos/CORBIS
55: © Davies/Getty Images
58: © LANL/Photo Researchers, Inc.
59: © Burstein Collection/CORBIS
60: © Charles Falco/Photo Researchers, Inc.
61: © Bettmann/CORBIS
63: © Hank Morgan/UMass Amherst/Photo Researchers, Inc.
64: © David Grossman/Photo Researchers, Inc.

COVER IMAGES FROM LEFT:
Nuclear power station © Dianne Maire/Shutterstock.com
Airplane © AbleStock.com
Golden Gate Bridge © Rick Parsons/Shutterstock.com